YOU
PROMISED, LORD

YOUNG READERS

YOU PROMISED, LORD

Prayers for Boys

Ron Klug

AUGSBURG Publishing House • Minneapolis

YOU PROMISED, LORD

Library of Congress Catalog Card No. 83-70502
International Standard Book No. 0-8066-2008-0

Scripture quotations unless otherwise noted are from the
Good News Bible, Today's English Version: copyright ©
American Bible Society 1966, 1971, 1976. Used by permission.

Photos: Rohn Engh, 15; Alan Cliburn, 23; Paul S. Conklin,
34; Richard West, 45; Norma Weinberg—Photo Marketing
Unlimited, 52; Focus on You, 59; C. Steven Short, 65;
Jean-Claude LeJeune, 73; Rollin M. Kocsis, 78.

Manufactured in the United States of America

For Blake
Chris and Ben
Phil and Andy
who helped
and for Paul and Hans

Contents

How to use this book

Joshua was a great soldier. He led the people of Israel into their promised land. He fought the battle of Jericho when the walls came tumbling down. He helped God's people defeat their enemies.

At the end of his life Joshua reminded God's people: "The Lord your God has given you all the good things that he promised. Every promise he made has been kept; not one has failed" (Joshua 23:14).

God has given you many promises too. You can find them in the Bible. God has promised you help, advice, healing, strength, forgiveness, and many other good things.

Because you have God's promises, you can pray with confidence. In this book you will find some of the best of God's promises and some prayers to help you talk to God about your life, your feelings, your problems, your questions.

Build your prayers on these promises of God. Copy out your favorite promises. Put them in your desk or in your locker. Write them on a poster or bookmark. Memorize them. Say them before you go to sleep and when you wake up. As you do this, your faith will grow and you will see God working in your life.

How can you know that God will keep his promises? Many Christians have trusted these promises and have found that God has helped them. But you will learn this for yourself only by trying God out, by trusting God's promises and asking for God's help.

Only remember: God has promised to give us everything we *need,* not necessarily everything we *want.* If you pray for a video game or a motorcycle, one will not necessarily turn up at your house the next morning. God knows what is really good for you.

And don't expect instant success. Prayer is not like putting money into a candy machine and pulling the handle. God has his own timing. Sometimes God does answer us very quickly, but other times we have to learn to wait for God.

One other thing to keep in mind: prayer is not a substitute for doing what you can do. It may not do much good to pray for help with a test if you haven't studied. When you are doing what you are able to, you can expect God to help you according to his promise.

The prayers in this book were written to help you talk to God about your life, your problems, your feelings. Not all the prayers will be exactly right for you. Feel free to change them so they say what you want to say. Then maybe you can go on and talk to God in your own words.

As you learn to pray, trusting in God's promises, you will be able to say with a writer of long ago: "The Lord is faithful to his promises, and everything he does is good" (Psalm 145:13).

Peace is what I leave with you; it is my own peace
that I give you. *John 14:27*

I feel nervous

I feel so nervous, Lord,
as jumpy as a rabbit.
I can't sit still.
I can't concentrate on anything.
I want to run and run and run.
I feel like I'm ready to fly apart into pieces.
Hold me together, Lord.
Calm me down.
Let me know the peace you promised, Jesus,
the quiet feeling deep inside me,
your peace,
your peace always.

I have the strength to face all conditions by the power Christ gives me.   *Philippians 4:13*

Help me today

Lord, help me today
to finish my chores at home without grumbling,
to try to make others happy,
to do my best in school,
to play by the rules and not get angry at others,
to give all the help I can,
to get along with my brothers and sisters,
to make the best of whatever happens,
to follow Jesus today
and do what he would do.
I ask this in his name.

I will be with you always, to the end of the
age.   *Matthew 28:20*

So alone

I feel so alone,
even in the middle of a crowded classroom
or a gym full of kids.
Right now nobody seems to be my friend.
There doesn't seem to be anybody
I can really talk to.
Lord, you've promised to be with me always.
Help me believe that.
Let me feel your presence,
and even when I can't feel it,
help me believe in it.
Thanks, Lord, for always being with me.

I pray to you, O Lord;
you hear my voice in the morning.   Psalm 5:2-3

Good morning, Lord

Good morning, Lord.
Thanks for a good night's sleep.
Be with me all through this day.
Be with me on the way to school:
take care of me and keep me out of trouble.
Be with me at school:
even when the work is hard or boring,
help me do my best.
Be with me on the playground and in the gym:
let me get along with my friends
and play fairly and safely.
Be with me at home:
help me obey my parents
and get along with my family.

The Lord will guard you;
he is by your side to protect you.   *Psalm 121:5*

I get scared

Lord, sometimes I get scared.
I worry about getting beat up on the way to school.
I think about getting hit by a car.
I wonder what would happen
if our house caught on fire
or if there was a nuclear war.
I don't like to be scared,
but sometimes I can't help it.
Even when I don't have much courage, Lord,
I know you are by my side.
Help me trust you
and believe you are protecting me.

You are good to us and forgiving, full of constant love for all who pray to you.   *Psalm 86:5*

Evening prayer

Thank you, Lord,
for everything good that happened today
and for all your help and protection.
Forgive me for the wrongs I have done:
if I have gotten into trouble at school,
if I have been lazy,
if I have worried my parents,
if I have spoken words that hurt others,
if I have wasted my time,
if I have been selfish,
if I have grumbled or complained,
if I have been a bad example to others.
For Jesus' sake
forgive the wrong things I've done
and the good I've failed to do.
Help me tomorrow to do what is right.
Help me do what I can
to make life easier for everyone I meet.

If you see your brother commit a sin that does not
lead to death, you should pray to God,
who will give him life.   *1 John 5:16*

My friend in trouble

Lord, I'm worried about my friend.
He's really messing up,
and I'm afraid he's going to be in big trouble.
I don't know how to help him.
I can't tell on him,
but I don't want him
to keep on doing what he's doing.
Show me what I can do.
And will you please help him?
He needs you.

Your word is a lamp to guide me
and a light for my path.   *Psalm 119:105*

The Word of God

People tell me the Bible is the Word of God,
but I'm not sure what that means.
I like some parts of the Bible,
but other parts seem boring
because I can't understand them.
Lord, help me understand the Bible better.
Teach me what you want me to know.
Show me how to live.
Thank you especially
that through the Bible
I can get to know Jesus.

The Lord guides a man in the way he should go and protects those who please him.
If they fall, they will not stay down, because the Lord will help them up.   *Psalm 37:23-24*

A rotten day

Lord, this has been a rotten day.
I tripped in the lunch line and dumped a tray.
I forgot to study for a spelling test.
I missed an easy pop fly,
and everybody yelled at me.
Now I feel clumsy and stupid.
I don't think anybody likes me.
I don't like myself.
Lord, help me believe that you love me,
and let that make a difference in my life.
Help me love myself at little.
Pick me up again, Lord,
and please make tomorrow better.

Give yourself to the Lord;
trust in him, and he will help you.   *Psalm 37:5*

Before a test

There's a big test coming up, Lord.
I've studied hard,
but I still don't feel ready.
Help me when I take the test.
Keep me from being so nervous
that I forget what I studied.
Help me think clearly and do my best.
I trust your promise, Lord.
I know you'll be helping me.
I'll be counting on that, Lord.
Help me pass the test.

I say to the Lord, "You are my Lord; all the
good things I have come from you."   *Psalm 16:2*

Thanks for friends

Lord, I thank you for my friends.
We enjoy
playing ball,
shooting baskets,
trading stamps,
drawing pictures,
riding bikes,
playing games,
going fishing,
laughing together,
or just talking.
I'm thankful you've given me these friends to enjoy.
Help us be good friends always.

You will show me the path that leads to life;
your presence fills me with joy and
brings me pleasure forever.   *Psalm 16:11*

I'm bored

God, I'm bored.
I don't know what to do.
There's nothing to do around here
that's any fun.
I wish something different
or exciting
would happen.
Keep me from getting into trouble
looking for excitement.
Please give me a good idea for something to do.
Show me how to use this time.

I urge that petitions, prayers, requests, and thanksgivings be offered to God for all people; for kings and all others who are in authority, that we may live a quiet and peaceful life.   *1 Timothy 2:1-2*

Help the leaders

I wonder what it's like
to be president of the United States.
Maybe it would be fun to be that famous and powerful,
to fly around in your own jet
and be on TV
But it must be tough.
He has so much responsibility
and has to make hard decisions.
Be with the president, Lord,
and all those who work with him.
Make them wise enough
and kind enough
to do the right thing.
Remind us to pray for them
and not just criticize.
Help the other leaders in the world too,
so they all work together to end war
so we can live in peace
as your children.

"Respect your father and mother" is the first
commandment that has a promise added: "so that
all may go well with you, and you may live
a long time in the land."   *Ephesians 6:2-3*

I'm growing up

I wish mom would stop treating me like a baby.
She tells me how to do everything.
She makes me wear boots and a cap
when none of the other boys do.
Then I get teased.
She says, "Drink your milk," and
"Eat your vegetables. They're good for you."
I wish she'd stop fussing at me.
I guess she does it because she cares about me
and wants me to be healthy and safe.
But I still get tired of it.
Help me do what she says
without complaining.
And please help mom see
that I'm growing up.

We know that in all things God works for good
with those who love him, those whom he has called
according to his purpose.   *Romans 8:28*

God works for good

Why has this bad thing happened, Lord?
It makes me wonder if you care about us.
I feel alone and hurt.
I guess bad things happen in the world,
even to your people.
Lord, you've promised
that even in the worst situation
you are working for our good.
Help me believe that.
Bring some good out of this bad situation, God.
I know that nothing
can ever separate me from your love.
I'm counting on that, Lord.

I am the Lord, the one who heals you.

Exodus 15:26

Tired of being sick

I'm tired of being sick, God.
At first it was fun
to stay home from school.
But now I'm bored.
The TV programs during the day are terrible,
and I'm tired of reading.
I'd like to be able to play
the way I always do.
I miss my friends.
Thank you for the help I'm getting
from doctors and nurses,
the medicine I'm taking,
and my parents, who are taking care of me.
Heal me, Lord,
according to your promise.

If any of you lacks wisdom, he should pray to God,
who will give it to him; because God gives
generously and graciously to all.   *James 1:5*

How to act

Lord, how am I supposed to know how to act?
My parents tell me one thing.
The teacher says something else.
My friends have a different idea.
On TV people act another way.
How can I know what's right for me?
Lord, you know,
and you've promised to show me.
Help me hear you
inside me,
in the Bible,
through other people.
Teach me how to sort out all the ideas.
Help me make the best decisions I can
knowing that if I make a mistake,
you will forgive me
and help me start over.

God . . . generously gives us everything
for our enjoyment.   *1 Timothy 6:17*

For enjoyment

Thanks, God
for everything that makes my life enjoyable:
for books, television, and movies,
for art and music,
for sports and games,
for computers and video games,
for trips and vacations,
for parties and special meals,
for parks and forests,
for rivers and lakes.
Lord, you want our lives to be filled with joy.
Thank you for these gifts.

The Lord is near to those who are discouraged;
he saves those who have lost all hope. *Psalm 34:18*

I don't want to go to school

God, I don't want to go to school.
I'm tired of
assignments,
boring classes,
crabby teachers,
mean kids,
and noisy hallways.
I don't even like gym class or lunch period.
I don't always feel this way,
but I do now.
Remind me of the good times, Lord.
I know I need to learn
and that not everything can be fun all the time.
Help me keep going,
and please make school fun again.

He helps us in all our troubles, so that we are
able to help others who have all kinds of troubles,
using the same help that we ourselves
have received from God.   *2 Corinthians 1:4*

So many hurting people

Lord, there are so many hurting people in the world.
I think of all those who are sick:
Lord, take away their pain and heal them.
I think of those who are poor and hungry:
Lord, supply them with food.
I think of all the handicapped people:
Lord, give them strength and patience.
I think of those who live
where there is war and fighting:
Lord, give them peace.
I think of myself and my family:
help us when we have problems,
and show us how we can help others.

I will always guide you
and satisfy you with good things.
I will keep you strong and well.   *Isaiah 58:11*

The people in my life

O Lord, bless the important people in my life.
Bless my parents:
take care of them so they can care for us.
Bless my brothers and sisters:
help us live together in happy and helpful ways.
Bless my grandparents and other relatives:
thank you for making me part of a big family.
Bless my friends:
help us be good friends to each other
in school and when we're playing.
Bless my pastor and teachers:
through them teach me what I need to know.
Bless all those in my community.
that make my life safe, healthy, and enjoyable. Amen.

If I flew away beyond the east
or lived in the farthest place in the west,
you would be there to lead me,
you would be there to help me.   *Psalm 139:9-10*

Why do we have to move?

My parents say we're moving.
I don't want to go.
I like it here.
I don't want to lose my friends.
I hate being the new kid in the neighborhood,
the one in school who doesn't know what's going on.
What if I don't like it in the new place?
Maybe I won't have any friends.
Why can't we just stay where we are?
I have so many questions.
There's so much I don't know.
But I do know that you'll be there, God.
You've promised that wherever I go
you'll be there to lead me and help me.
I'll be trusting that promise, Lord.

Be kind and tender-hearted to one another,
and forgive one another, as God has
forgiven you through Christ.   *Ephesians 4:32*

Now we're not friends

My friend and I got into a fight,
and now we're not friends anymore.
We used to have really good times together;
I could talk to him about anything.
But now I can't stand him,
and he won't even look at me.
It seems foolish, Lord.
I'm still mad,
but now it doesn't seem as important.
I'd like to be his friend again,
but I don't know how.
Forgive us for fighting, Lord.
Help me to say I'm sorry.
Give me the courage to smile first.
And help my friend understand
that I want to be friends again.

Praise the Lord, my soul,
and do not forget how kind he is . . .
He fills my life with good things,
so that I stay young and strong
like an eagle.   *Psalm 103:2, 5*

Lord, you've been good

Lord, you have been good to me in so many ways.
For my parents and a safe, loving home,
I thank you, Lord.
For my school and teachers and the chance to learn,
I thank you, Lord.
For my friends and the good times we have together,
I thank you, Lord.
For good books, games, sports, movies, and TV,
I thank you, Lord.
For my pastor and Sunday school teachers,
I thank you, Lord.
Help me to be always thankful
for these and all your good gifts.
Remind me to share with others,
so they can be thankful too.

So let us not become tired of doing good;
for if we do not give up, the time will come
when we will reap the harvest.   *Galatians 6:9*

Why do they pick on me?

Why do my parents pick on me all the time?
Why do they have to find fault with everything I do?
If I do everything right except one small thing,
they mention the thing that was wrong,
and never what I've done right.
I get so tired of it.
Sometimes I just feel like giving up.
Why should I try,
when I know I'll never be good enough?
I guess they mean well.
They want me to grow up right.
Help me understand that.
And help my parents understand
that sometimes I need to hear
I'm doing something right.
Give me patience
and the willingness to keep on trying.

Leave all your worries with him,
because he cares for you.   *1 Peter 5:7*

I worry about so many things

I worry about so many things, Lord.
What will I do if I have to go to the bathroom
on a field trip?
What would happen if lightning hit our house
while I was watching TV?
What would we do if dad got cancer?
When I take the bus downtown,
will I get lost?
What will the teacher do
if I'm sick when we have a test?
If I got my hand stuck in the freezer,
would it freeze and fall off?
Sometimes when I talk about my worries,
my family laughs at me.
That only makes it worse.
Maybe some of my worries *are* a little silly.
Most of these disasters don't happen.
Help me keep my head on straight.
Let me give these worries to you, Lord.
I know you've promised to care for me always.

It is the Lord who gives wisdom;
from him come knowledge
and understanding.   *Proverbs 2:6*

Our school

Lord, bless our school today.
Be with the principal and administrators:
help them make good plans and wise decisions.
Be with the teachers:
give them patience and kindness.
Be with the librarians:
let them help us find good books and other materials.
Be with school bus drivers, cooks,
custodians, and secretaries:
may they help make school safe and pleasant.
Be with all the students:
may we study hard, learn well, and help one another.

For the Spirit that God has given us does not make us timid; instead, his Spirit fills us with power, love, and self-control.   *2 Timothy 1:7*

What do I do now?

I hate having to meet new people,
especially adults.
I never know what to say
or what to do.
It's not that I want to be impolite,
but I'm not sure what's expected of me,
and I can't think of anything to say.
Then I feel self-conscious and embarrassed.
When I walk into a room full of people,
I feel as if everybody is looking at me.
That's hard too.
Will I ever get over feeling so self-conscious?
Lord, help me know how to act and what to do.
Give me more confidence
in meeting people.

When you pass through deep waters,
I will be with you; your troubles
will not overwhelm you.   *Isaiah 43:2*

Living with pain

Lord, it's hard to live with this pain.
It hurts all the time.
Sometimes I'm not sure I can stand it.
Lord, help.
I need your strength.
Make me strong enough.
Take away the pain.
Help me be well again.

Everything that happens in this world happens
at the time God chooses.   *Ecclesiastes 3:1*

Being grown-up

I wish I could grow up faster.
I'd like to be taller
and have bigger muscles.
I wish I could drive a motorcycle
and stay up as late as I want.
I'd like to be able to go anywhere I want to
and eat what I feel like eating.
Sometimes it's not much fun being a kid.
But there are some good things about now.
I can stay up later than I used to.
I can go downtown by myself.
I can play ball better than last year.
I have a good place to live.
My parents take care of me.
I have enough time to play.
Help me enjoy life now, Lord.
I know I'm growing up
at the pace that's right for me.

We know that God, who raised the Lord Jesus to life,
will also raise us up with Jesus and take us,
together with you, into his presence.

2 Corinthians 4:14

When you die

Death is scary.
I don't like to think about it,
but sometimes I wonder what it feels like
and what happens when you die.
I think about what would happen
if my parents would die,
or if I would.
Sometimes I try to imagine
what heaven will be like.
Lord, you haven't answered all our questions
about life and death,
but we know that Jesus died and rose from death
so that when we die
we will live with you
forever.

Do not forget to do good and to help
one another, because these are the
sacrifices that please God. *Hebrews 13:16*

Someone needs a friend

Everyone picks on this kid in class.
They're always hiding his books
or tripping him
or teasing him.
Nobody wants to sit next to him
because he's different.
Sometimes I'm mean to him too.
I know it's not right,
but I don't want to be one of those on the outside.
Forgive me, Jesus.
When you were on earth
you didn't care only
for the strong and popular people.
You were friends with the poor
and the people nobody else liked.
Help me be like that.
Give me the courage to be a friend
to those who really need one.

God is always at work in you
to make you willing and able to obey
his own purpose.   *Philippians 2:13*

Doing hard things

O Lord, help me today
to do the things that are hard for me:
to keep trying
when I feel like giving up;
to do what's right
when others are doing wrong;
to obey parents and teachers
when I'd like to have my own way;
to be kind
when I feel like being mean;
to study
when I'd rather watch TV or play;
to do my chores at home
even when I don't feel like it;
to forgive others
when I've been cheated or hurt.
These things are hard for me.
I can't do them on my own.
Lord, you've promised
that you are always at work inside me.
I believe that with your help
I can do these hard things.

O Lord, our Lord, your greatness is seen
in all the world!   *Psalm 8:9*

Robots and rockets

Are there really flying saucers and E.T.s?
I wonder about that sometimes.
I like to learn about space and rockets
and robots and black holes
and galaxies and space shuttles.
Thanks for giving us such an exciting universe
to study and explore.
And thanks for minds that can learn and think.
Lord, the whole universe shows us your greatness!

Don't take it on yourself to repay a wrong.
Trust in the Lord and he will make it right.
Proverbs 20:22

My sister!

Sometimes I wish my sister didn't live with us.
She gets good grades
and makes me look bad.
She corrects me every time I make a mistake.
She teases me
and gets me into trouble.
I know I'm supposed to love her
because she's my sister,
but it sure is hard.
I know you've made us part of the same family, Lord.
Please give me a better feeling about her,
and help us get along with each other.

If we confess our sins to God, he will keep
his promise and do what is right;
he will forgive us our sins and purify us
from all our wrongdoing.   *1 John 1:9*

I'm selfish

Lord, sometimes I'm selfish.
I don't want to share.
I want my own way.
I act as if I'm the only one who counts.
I know this is wrong,
that you ask us to care for other people
the way you care for us.
I'm glad that you forgive me
and that you can change me.
Help me to think of others
and not just myself.
Teach me to share.

There is nothing in all creation that will
ever be able to separate us from the love of God
which is ours through Christ Jesus
our Lord.   *Romans 8:39*

What will the future bring?

I wonder what the world will be like in the future.
Will robots do the work for us?
Will we fly to the moon on rockets?
Will there be enough food for everyone?
Will there be war?
I have so many questions about the future,
and nobody knows the answers for sure,
but I like to think about it.
Sometimes I'm excited about the future
and what I'll be able to do.
Other times I worry about it.
Lord, you've promised
that whatever the future brings
you'll be there;
nothing will be able to separate me from your love.
Help me believe that.

The laws of the Lord are right,
and those who obey them are happy.   *Psalm 19:8*

All those rules

Sometimes I wish I belonged to a different family,
where I could watch whatever TV programs I want,
where I could have money to buy everything I want,
where I could eat all the junk food I want,
where I could always stay up as late as I want.
Why do my parents make so many rules?
Why can't I just do what I feel like doing?
Would that be better for me, Lord?
I know my parents think the rules are good for me.
You gave us laws and commandments too, Lord,
to show us how we can live
in ways that will make us happy.
Help me recognize that good rules are helpful,
and help my parents see that sometimes
I need to make my own decisions.

God has said, "I will never leave you;
I will never abandon you."   *Hebrews 13:5*

Divorce

Lord, it's not easy having parents who are divorced.
It's hard being part of two families.
Sometimes I get angry at my parents.
I wish they could have found a way to get along
without splitting up the family.
I know it wasn't my fault.
Lord, forgive my parents
wherever they've done wrong.
Help me forgive them.
Show me how to love and help both of them.
Let me believe that no matter what happens,
you will never leave me.
You will love and care for me
always.

Remember the Lord in everything you do,
and he will show you the right way.   *Proverbs 3:6*

My, how you've grown!

Why do grown-ups say,
"My, how you've grown!"?
When we go on vacation
I must hear it a hundred times.
My aunts say it.
My grandma says it.
Their neighbors say it.
Why can't they ask me
what I've been reading
or whether I like math
or how my baseball team is doing?
How can you answer politely to
"My, how you've grown!"?
It's hard to think of anything at all to say,
so I just stand there and feel dumb.
I'm thankful I'm growing,
but please help adults notice
something more interesting about me,
like how fast I can run
or how well I can play the piano
or catch a football.

At the time you are put to the test,
he will give you strength to endure it, and so
provide you with a way out.   *1 Corinthians 10:13*

Going along

It's easy, Lord, to do what everybody else is doing.
I want to be liked.
I want to have friends.
I don't want the other kids to think I'm weird.
But I also want to do what you want.
How do I put the two together?
Sometimes I pretend to be something I'm not
just so they'll like me.
I laugh at things that aren't funny
and pretend to enjoy things I don't really like.
Give me the courage to do
what I know you want me to do.
Give me friends who will make it easier for me
to do what's right.

When you pray, I will answer you.
When you call to me, I will respond.   *Isaiah 58:9*

When I pray

Lord, you've promised that when I pray
you will always hear my prayer
and answer me.
Sometimes I'm sure of that,
but other times it seems
as if I'm talking to myself.
When I pray,
help me believe that you will answer me,
even if I don't feel any different.
Make me a strong believer, Lord.

Seek your happiness in the Lord, and he
will give you your heart's desire.   *Psalm 37:4*

Winning the game

Tomorrow is our big game.
I sure hope we win.
We're all going to try.
Winning feels good,
and I don't like to lose.
Help us win, Lord.
Is it all right for me to ask that?
Maybe I should just ask that
we play as well as we can
and that nobody gets hurt.
But if it's all right with you,
I'd still like to win.

If you endure suffering even when
you have done right,
God will bless you for it.   *1 Peter 2:20*

It's not fair!

It's not fair, Lord.
I'm being punished for something I didn't do.
Why does everyone think I did it?
Nobody believes me.
I'm hurt,
and I'm mad!
Even if the others never believe me,
Lord, you know I didn't do it.
Make me strong enough to take this
without hurting anyone.
It it's possible,
bring some good out of this.

Happy are those who work for peace;
God will call them his children!   *Matthew 5:9*

Give peace, Lord

Why is there so much fighting in the world?
Sometimes I like to play war,
but I know that in a real war
homes are bombed,
families are separated,
and people are hurt and killed.
Why do there have to be wars?
Why can't people just get along?
Lord, show me what I can do to be a peacemaker
in my family,
my neighborhood,
my country,
the world.
Give peace among nations,
peace in our homes,
and peace in our hearts.

Whoever sees me sees also him
who sent me.   *John 12:45*

Thanks for Jesus

Sometimes, God, I can feel you are near me,
but I can't see you.
I'm glad that Jesus came to earth
to show us what you are like.
He helped people.
He healed the sick.
He fed the hungry.
He forgave people.
Thank you, God,
that Jesus came to live with us
and that he died and rose again
to show us your love for us
and your power over death.

Whatever you do, work at it with all your heart,
as though you were working for the Lord
and not for men. Remember that the Lord
will give you as a reward what he has
kept for his people.   *Colossians 3:23-24*

I don't like my teacher

I don't like my teacher, Lord.
She's mean to us.
She doesn't explain things right.
She makes me feel dumb all the time.
She never gives us a break.
I wish I had the teacher I had last year.
She helped us learn
and even made school seem like fun.
Thanks for the good teachers, Lord.
Help me live with this one.
Remind me to do my schoolwork for you, Lord.

The message about Christ's death on the cross
is nonsense to those who are being lost;
but for us who are being saved
it is God's power.   *1 Corinthians 1:18*

A bad temper

Lord, I know I have a bad temper.
Sometimes I get really mad
and then I want to smash something
or someone.
Sometimes I'm in a bad mood
and I don't even know why.
Show me how to handle these feelings, God,
without hurting someone else
or myself.
Forgive me, Lord
and make me strong enough
to be more patient and forgiving.

I have come in order that you might have life—
life in all its fullness.   *John 10:10*

Thanks for my parents

Lord, I like it when my parents
do fun things with me—
hiking in the park,
baking cookies,
going on vacation,
reading together,
going to a movie,
eating pizza,
or just having a long talk.
Thanks for these good times we have together.
I'm lucky to have parents who care.
When things don't always go exactly right at home,
help me remember the good times.
Thanks for my parents.
Take care of them,
and thanks for making us a family.

And with all his abundant wealth
through Christ Jesus, my God will
supply all your needs.   *Philippians 4:19*

Enough money?

The TV says many people are out of work.
We don't seem to have enough money to pay the bills.
I worry about what will happen to us
and to all the other people.
O God, you've promised to take care of us.
You don't promise to give us everything we want,
but you did promise to give us
everything we really need.
You know what we need, Lord.
Help us trust you for it.

Love your enemies and pray for those who
persecute you, so that you may become the
sons of your Father in heaven.   *Matthew 5:44-45*

They don't like me

Lord, there are some kids at school
who don't like me.
I don't know why.
They like to hurt me any way they can.
They call me names,
they push me around,
they laugh at me.
I'm afraid of them.
Jesus, you had enemies too.
You know what it means to be hurt.
You prayed for your enemies,
and died to make them your friends.
Show me what to do in this situation.
Give me courage for each day.

It is one and the same Spirit who does all this;
as he wishes, he gives a different gift
to each person.   *1 Corinthians 12:11*

What am I good at?

How come everybody seems better than I am?
Why do I do so many things wrong?
The Bible says
you give gifts and abilities to everyone, Lord,
that we're all good at something.
Help me know what I'm good at.
Remind me that I don't have to compare myself
with others.
Let me feel good about being me.

You will seek me, and you will find me
because you will seek me
with all your heart.   *Jeremiah 29:13*

Looking for God

You promised that if I really look for you,
I will find you.
Help me know where to look.
Help me learn more about you
in church,
in the Bible,
through my friends and family,
through the world you have made.
And help me believe
that you are always looking for me too.

God has made us what we are, and in our union
with Christ Jesus he has created us
for a life of good deeds, which he has
already prepared for us to do.   *Ephesians 2:10*

Why am I so dumb?

Why am I so dumb, Lord?
I hate to read in front of the class
because everybody else reads better than I do.
Some kids have finished their math
when I'm still stuck on the second problem.
I study more than they do,
but they get the A's
when I'm lucky to get a C.
Why didn't you make me smarter?
Help me, Lord,
to be thankful for what you have given me.
You've made me what I am.
Help me use the abilities I have
without comparing myself to others.
Let me be satisfied with being me.

The Lord says, "I will teach you
the way you should go; I will instruct
and advise you."   *Psalm 32:8*

What should I be?

I don't know what I want to be
when I grow up.
Some kids have plans already.
They seem to have a clear idea
of where they're going,
but I sure don't.
Sometimes I think I want to be an astronaut,
or a baseball player,
or a musician,
or a doctor,
or a missionary,
or a scientist.
How can I know what is right for me?
What do you want me to do, Lord?
I know I don't have to decide right now.
Help me trust in you to show me, little by little,
the way I should go.
Let me find work that will be right for me
and helpful to other people.

If the Son sets you free,
then you will be really free. *John 8:36*

Bad habits

Bad habits are hard to break, Lord.
I have a bad habit,
and I make up my mind not to do it.
I even promise you that I'll stop.
But I slip back into it again.
Then I get mad at myself for being so weak.
Forgive me, Lord,
and help me accept your forgiveness.
Set me free from this habit
and let me go on living with confidence.

The Lord is my light and my salvation;
I will fear no one.   *Psalm 27:1*

Being laughed at

More than anything in the world
I hate being laughed at.
I don't like to mess up,
especially in front of other kids.
I hate being teased and put down.
It makes me feel like a nothing
Lord, you've said I'm worth something,
even when I fail.
Don't let me be so afraid of being laughed at
that I won't try.
Help me get over this fear of what others think.
Make me so strong on the inside
that I won't worry about it any more.

He heals the broken-hearted
and bandages their wounds.   *Psalm 147:3*

I'm disappointed

I'm so disappointed!
I wanted something so much,
but I didn't get it.
Why don't things work out the way we want?
I even prayed about it.
Now I feel let down.
Help me get over this feeling.
There must be some reason this didn't work out.
Maybe you have something better planned for me.
I hope so.
I don't understand right now,
but I know you'll take care of things.
You''ll answer my prayer in your own way.
Thank you, God.

You will listen, O Lord, to the prayers of the lowly;
you will give them courage.   *Psalm 10:17*

Thanks for listening

Nobody listens to me.
They think I'm just a kid.
They're too busy with their own lives
to pay any attention to me.
Lord, you've promised to listen,
and I know I can always talk to you
when I can't talk to anyone else.
I know I can talk about anything to you
and that you will hear me
and help me.
Thanks, Lord.

The Lord is good;
his love is eternal and his faithfulness
lasts forever.   *Psalm 100:5*

Today I feel great!

Everything seems to be going right today.
I feel good about myself.
I'm happy with my family.
Things are going well at school.
I'm getting along with my friends.
You've given me so much, Lord:
home and family,
friends,
a beautiful world to explore.
I feel great just being alive!
Thank you, Lord.